Exercising

by Robin Nelson

Series consultants: Sonja Green, MD, and
Distinguished Professor Emerita Ann Nolte, PhD,
Department of Health Sciences, Illinois State University

Lerner Publications Company • Minneapolis

Lerner Publications Company
A division of Lerner Publishing Group
241 First Avenue North
Minneapolis, MN 55401 U.S.A.

Website address: www.lernerbooks.com

Words in **bold type** are explained in a glossary on page 31.

Library of Congress Cataloging-in-Publication Data

Nelson, Robin, 1971–
    Exercising / by Robin Nelson.
      p. cm. – (Pull ahead books)
    Includes index.
    ISBN-13: 978-0-8225-3489-1 (lib. bdg. : alk. paper)
    ISBN-10: 0-8225-3489-4 (lib. bdg. : alk. paper)
    1. Exercise–Juvenile literature. 2. Exercise–Health aspects–Juvenile literature. I. Title. II. Series.
    RA781.N53 2006
    613.7'1–dc22   2005017969

Manufactured in the United States of America
1 2 3 4 5 6 – JR – 11 10 09 08 07 06

Run, jump, skip, and climb!
How do you **exercise**?

Do you play a sport?
Do you ride a bike?

Do you jump rope?
Do you walk your dog?

There are many ways to exercise.

Every time you move your body, you are exercising.

Everybody needs to exercise. Exercise keeps our bodies **healthy** and strong.

When you exercise, you are using your **muscles**. Your muscles make your body move. The more you exercise, the stronger your muscles get.

Your muscles need **energy** to work. Where do you get energy? You get energy when you eat healthy food.

You get energy when you get enough sleep.

You also need **oxygen** to exercise.
Oxygen is in the air that you breathe.

That is why you start to breathe deeper and faster when you exercise. Your body is trying to get more oxygen to your muscles.

Your heart is a muscle. It pumps blood through your body. The blood carries energy and oxygen.

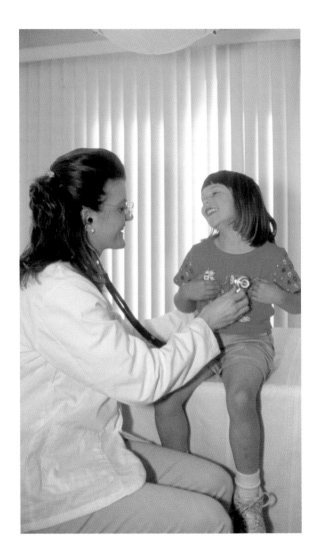

Exercise is good for your heart. It keeps your heart strong. It helps your heart pump blood.

Did you know that your body loses water when you exercise? It loses water when you sweat. Sweating helps you cool down.

Remember to drink water before, during, and after exercise. Start drinking water even before you feel thirsty!

What else should you do before you exercise? You need to stretch! Stretching loosens up your muscles so that you won't get hurt.

Stretching
after exercise
keeps your
muscles from
getting stiff.
If you forget
to stretch,
your body
might ache
the next day!

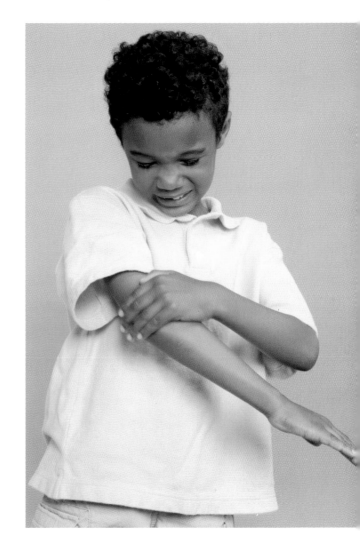

To stay healthy, you should exercise at least 60 minutes every day.

You can get your hour of activity throughout the day.

You could ice-skate or shoot hoops.

You could swim or dance. You could go hiking or play kickball.

You can exercise alone or with a friend.

You can exercise indoors or outdoors.

Exercise can be fun! It can make you feel good about yourself.

It also makes
you stronger.
Exercise
helps keep
you healthy!

Exercise Tips

■ Drink lots of water before, during, and after exercise.

■ Walk or jog for a few minutes before you stretch your muscles.

■ Stop exercising if you feel sick or really warm.

■ Do different kinds of exercises each day.

■ Get up and move around at least once an hour.

■ Walk or bike to places whenever you can.

How Do You Exercise?

How many of these things did you do today? What other kinds of exercise did you get?

baseball	golf	raking leaves
basketball	gymnastics	running
biking	hockey	skateboarding
building a snowperson	hopscotch	skiing
canoeing	ice skating	skipping
chores	in-line skating	sledding
climbing	jumping jacks	soccer
dancing	jump rope	swimming
field hockey	karate	swinging
flying a kite	kickball	tag
football	playing catch	tennis
four square	playing on the playground	tug-of-war
Frisbee	pull-ups	volleyball
gardening	push-ups	walking
		yoga

More about Exercising

Books

Brunhoff, Laurent de. *Babar's Yoga for Elephants.* New York: Harry N. Abrams, 2002.

Gray, Shirley W. *Exercising for Good Health.* Chanhassen, MN: The Child's World, 2004.

Johnson, Rebecca L. *The Muscular System.* Minneapolis: Lerner Publications Company, 2005.

Mitchell, Melanie. *Eating Well.* Minneapolis: Lerner Publications Company, 2006.

Silverstein, Alvin, Virginia Silverstein, and Laura Silverstein Nunn. *Physical Fitness.* New York: Franklin Watts, 2002.

Websites

BAM! Body and Mind
http://www.bam.gov/

Galaxy H
http://www.galaxy-h.gov.uk/your-body-and-activity.html

Get Kids in Action
http://www.getkidsinaction.org/kids/#home

KidsHealth
http://kidshealth.org/kid/

Glossary

energy: power within your body that lets you move and be active

exercise: moving your body so that your muscles keep or increase their strength

healthy: being in good condition physically and mentally or something that helps you stay in good condition

muscles: parts of your body that help you move

oxygen: a gas in the air that you breathe and that is necessary for life

Index

Photo Acknowledgments

The photographs in this book appear courtesy of: © Ariel Skelly/CORBIS, cover; © Royalty-Free/CORBIS, pp. 3, 4, 6, 10, 28; © age fotostock/SuperStock, pp. 5, 18; Brand X Pictures, pp. 7, 8, 20, 21, 23; © David Turnley/ CORBIS, p. 9; © SuperStock, p. 11; © K. Solveig/CORBIS, p. 12; © Richard Cummins, p. 13; © Diane M. Meyer, p. 14; © Lawrence Migdale/Photo Researchers, Inc., p. 15; © Gary Kufner/CORBIS, p. 16; © Mark Clarke/Photo Researchers, Inc., p. 17; © Todd Strand/Independent Picture Service, p. 19; © David Stoecklein/ CORBIS, p. 22; © Tom & Dee Ann McCarthy/CORBIS, p. 24; © Tony Demin/CORBIS, p. 25; EyeWire by Getty Images, pp. 26, 27.